push buttons and stir pots

by

bradley f koetting

PUSH BUTTONS AND STIR POTS by Bradley F. Koetting

Copyright © 2009 by Bradley Fredrick Koetting

Single Malt Press

PO Box 34

Timberon, NM 88350

bfkoetting@gmail.com

cover by Wild Card

Also by Bradley F. Koetting: *fisher of men, running out of fear*

ISBN - 978-0-578-04108-7

acknowledgements

Dios le bendice

The Good Lord, Jesus Christ, my loving, understanding mother, Jorge, Lin and David, Mary, Pito, Lee, my boat, Derbes, Chip, Goat, Mr. Card, Mr. Pink, my cats, Mongo, my dealer, Snelvis and Sherry, Ray, Coates, my toilet, my compressor, Lisa at Milagros in Del Rio, Billy, Martie, Greg and Lupe, Big Son The, Jennifer, Ryan, Mac, John, Pecan Acres Ranch, Regina, Don, Townes, R Bingham, Lawrence of Afaggia, Suzi, Dwyn, Bear, Beau, Birdman, Sue Dog, Boot, The Violator, Bouley, Sonia, Martha, C-Shot, Glenna, Fred, Teresa, Gary, Medicine Wolf, Ace, Becky, Braxton, Doc E, growers everywhere, all the righteous, my future PO, my scranus & all the kind nurses at Saint Joe's.

hey chuckie, go fuck yourself

*"and don't ever let them
make you feel
like saying what you want
is unbecoming*

*if you were supposed
to watch your mouth
all the time
i doubt your eyes
would be
above it"*

- Mike Cooley
  Drive-By Truckers
  "Gravity's Gone"

for Paul

poems

ranch rules
chip
faith
groin injury
pissed
lacuna
answers
walmarks
action
diarrhea 4
saloon
off to dc
few
father
gone
greed
stay
donkey dick
don't fuck me
passion
rattlesnake runs
bustle
score
time
hair
behave
love thy
difference
30 fishing poles
US
past due
whatever you say
nice
bull's eye
cutie
Mama Suzi
bitchin
forgotten
moon watch
dirty hatred
no regrets
constant

question
roid
smoke
going for broke
leaving on
funny
career
Pajaro
thread
con per miso
cards
one for the non believers
winged
sobriety
representative
bastard
blathering
whores
fly
713
dead animals
return
strike
wind
but i do
now
in love
mulligan
candle
nine
thanks
liar
saint Jude
spade
jump
the ok ranch
yesterday
7 dead Paisanos
sartorial thief
in a year
idiot
windex

ranch rules

nothin goes to waste
that's a ranch rule

don't come back to the truck without
something that eats or burns
or an arrowhead
that's also a ranch rule

always carry water
and
have at least two spare tires
these are both ranch rules too

leave it as you found it
or better
that's the golden ranch rule

and
since i can't obey
eleven simple Commandments

reckon i oughtta try
them ranch rules

they work better
because there's no
real
faith involved

chip

i'm not the one to decide
but my cousin
is
pretty smart

except
when he stole second base
with the bases loaded

twice

faith

God gifted us with passion
not just passion
but a passion

when you accept yours
you have found your happiness

don't let the misery
of chasing it down
keep you from the conquest

because that's what it is
a bloody smelly miserable war
dead dogs and rotting horses
lies and loss and hell eternal

there is no retreat for the insane
and what you seek you will not find
and the root of that pain is love

until you weather this storm
it won't stop raining

make it everything that you are
lock down the iron doors of madness
and stay a while

a long sacred while

and remember
you quit
you die

9/6/2009 2:13 PM – oknm

groin injury

neither
do i hurry
nor
do i worry

in the absence of one
so follows
the death of the other

time will not slow
it will not stop
it is earthly
unseen everything

to chase the elusive
is for the crazed
the sick
the homeless
the soul searchers
the foul speaking outlaws
and of course
all those
phonies

but they always
end up
dead
or dying
on their way
back
to the ant hill

it was both
the hurry
and
the worry

the entire trip
was a wasted life

pissed

my girlfriend accused me of being
incestuously gay

the supposed boyfriend being my cousin
he lives in the next town over

it's tough to break me
i was born a stone
grew into a rock
now i am a mountain

my ex-wife was the same
i had to call her a cunt
to get her to move out

the c bomb
it's a killer

so me and my cousin
were sixtynining each other out in the barn
sort of broke butt mountain style
spurs and hay and silk chaps flyin ever where

that's fucking funny

being accused of something
you ain't
is enough to bring a mighty mountain
to rubble and ruin

the accusation of incest
was just a bonus
a dog pissing on some gravel

more for us to laugh about really

why does this shit happen to me
we make sex practically every time we're together

not my cousin and me

lacuna

lately my thoughts have been very loud
they conquer the peripheral of my world
everything drowns in the screaming chaos
the world is just a bad television show

there's no evil
no good
there's no nothing

something's got me gone missin
i'm walking through the warm cobwebs
the casket is closed

just a simple little thought
a shooting star firing across the late dusk sky

it tears away my soul
and devours it

it's my dog sitting entranced on the bloody knife
awaiting the next scrap tossed from the carcass

what else could it be

answers

it's too quiet
my broken heart
pains to beat
my aching spirit
wanting to run
and fly away from here
forever

but there is nowhere to go
not right now

pussies and frenchmen run
not me
not now

it's only right to stay
to process the quiet
listen to the lessons
whispering in its winds

and the strands of faith
are invisible
i feel for them
but my hands are numb
and cold
and empty

i feel nothing
in this silence
but confusion
and eternal loss

another reason
to see no fairness
in this life

but i do have
the next one
to look forward to

action

if a man's known intent
is to kill you
what do you do
after
you have killed him

just think
you come into to contact with some freak
who decides
that it will thrill up
the hell in him
to kill you

you get lucky
and discover his plan

even before he's dead
your life too
has forever changed
and will be always be bound in darkness

thanks to destiny
to luck
to chance
to fortune
to the absence of them all

sometimes
we're left without a choice

but it's always choice
that leads us

walmarks

she was in front of me
in line at the pharmacy
gray roots climbing up
to orange curls of dying hair

3 dollars and 30 cents

then she busted out the check book

i could smell the smoke
billowing out of my ears

in the parking lot
she shoved away her empty cart
coasting into a cluster of others
blocking at least eight parking spots

not hesitating
i sounded out
my voice growing louder

that's where that goes
that's where that goes
that's where that fucking goes

as she tried to close the door
of her minitruck
i grabbed it
holding it open

she looked up at me
as if she were
about to be assaulted

hey lady
just because you're old and stupid
doesn't give you an excuse
to be lazy and inconsiderate

leave me alone mister

i'm about to
but i just wanted you to know

that people like you
are hemorrhoids on the asshole
of this animal we call
life

she slammed shut her door
nearly ripping off my fingers

then sped away in her little red truck
all the while
flipping me a crooked wrinkled finger

i laughed so hard that i vomited
that morning's screwdrivers
right there in the parking lot

are you okay young man

it was another old woman

i'm fine mam

are you sick

yes mam
i'm sick
sick and tired

i'm so sorry

don't be
no one else is

especially me

diarrhea 4

for some reason
some people
think they're
very well liked
when
in all actuality
they're irritating
phony cretinous
crap coated cow assses

why does a man
need an earring

i am so damn cute
i'm gonna decorate
myself
like a Christmas tree

hang a bulb
from my adorable ear
and turn the lights on

here i come
baby

good
keep going

fame to shame

and you
and others
have the sparkling proof

later in life
you'll try to blame it on youth
but you can't
your arrogance
simply
won't let you

saloon

it woke me last night
but i didn't write it down

i'll remember in the morning

and i actually did

the difference between
a cunt
and
a whore

a whore will steal your soul
while pretending to buy it

a cunt has no soul
because it's already been whored

of course

off to dc

she's going for a week
she said she was scared
of flying so far alone

it's not like flying to
Dallas or something
ya know

dc on independence day
twelve and angelic

i wished her well
she said that she loved me
and that she'd send pictures
i told her i loved her too
and to be careful

what i didn't tell her
was to do everything
see everything she can
soak in every detail around her
remember those who never
throughout the entirety of their lives
have ever left the village

and when you get back home
avoid those with shit on their faces
because those aren't the shit eaters
that you can see on the internet
these folks are different
they live in their own feces
they fuck in it
they can't see the world as you do
because they themselves are standing in the way

it's usually caused
by insecurity
by laziness
sucking on the tit
of self pity
and lots of people are
just plain crazy

find those truly humble ones

no one is without sin
but there are those
who have ceased casting stones

it's these souls
that see the utter self defeating
ineffectiveness
of fear and disgust

i once asked my brother
your father

how do all these
fucked up people
find each other

dirt finds dirt
he said

reckon that's why
i'm the outcast
of the family

but i've never had
anyone's shit
on my face

especially
not my own

few

the meek

blessed are they

blessed they truly are

selfless souls

you
are
so
outnumbered

father

from the age of 4
i was raised by a
trained assassin
retired of course

many times
were difficult
and bloody

at times
too much for
a young boy

now
at 40
most are just
broken memories
the rest
buried alive
lost and forgotten

but i won't
hang my hat
on what has
come and gone

i won't be disabled
because of this
or anything else
or anyone on this planet

i've been scared
i've been insecure
and i've lost
a lot of time
wrestling
twisted
unnecessary
anger

maybe it was all
meant to be

maybe not

but
please be careful
when we embrace

i could kiss
your warm face
or
break your
fucking
neck

gone

any
moment
of profundity
i might have found
in my lifetime
is lost
forever
in
a solid state
of
charred
smoking
blessed
black out

greed

that world out there

the one with the people
and the violence
and the chaos
and the swallowing selfishness

it's not real to me anymore
it's just a bad television show

repeat
repeat
repeat

i changed the channel
several years past
and
i'm not going back

ever

they're all
being greedy

so can i

11/15/2009 11:11 a11/p11 –ok

stay

fences were originally built to
keep livestock in

now they're built to keep people out

fucking thieves
third world fucks
stay on your side of the wall

stay

you fucking stay i said

stay dammit

good

no no no
stay
i said stay
stay

good
good stay

donkey dick

i passed out
in the bed closest to the door

we were somewhere in the hill country
around Kerrville maybe

the place had a kitchenette

we had deer sausage in the cooler
we were drunk and stoned and tired and hungry

i remember the lights dimming around his
wobbling silhouette as i went black

it was as if
without his knowledge
catching a glimpse
of the grim reaper from behind

then the smoke almost killed me
because that idiot fell asleep
with the sausage still sizzling in the skillet

when he threw the links out onto the highway
they were squashed immediately by a passing truck

i crawled from the bed
coughing my way
to the fresh air outside

thinking that i could have died
from sausage smoke asphyxiation

and a bumbling idiot's
great idea

don't fuck me

if you do fuck me
i will hunt you down
like a gut shot deer
in the middle of the West Texas desert

then i'll beat you to death with chiseled fists
hold you by your jafro
and remove your head with a dull pocket knife
and kick it like a football
just for having to take the time

spring has come and the Turkey Vultures are here
so i'd cover your sorry carcass with Mojave snake bites
and the birds would have you to bones in days
bones which i would smash to dust
sprinkle atop my whiskey
drink down
and piss you out onto the fires of hell

you know i love you to death
but i don't want to

it's your choice

but i advise
not fucking me
my good friend

it would be a shame to miss you so much

passion

if you're gonna
head that direction
you might as well
go all the way

that location that doesn't
read on any compass
a position that holds no stillness
and cannot be detected

a fool's trail to many
chasing a star across the sky

a friend once said

writer
huh
the easy way out

he's a surgeon now
spending money
instead of time

some people get a helping hand
some get handled in awful ways
either way
deal with it

i'm still writing
and will be until the end

it's being bought right now
the price is everything and ugly
but
it will be paid for

when it comes to passion
even drunks like me
don't have time to waste

rattlesnake runs

i step into the fall night
the stars like rain
upon my shoulders
the evening air
eternal creosote

the coyotes drag away
a headless Jackrabbit
i wonder if the
venom
in its meat
will kill them too

this morning it was
you and the rabbit
he had no chance

this evening
it was you and me
had you not the hare
in your belly
i'd a died in my laziness

but finally you rattled
set off by Bruno's
youthful curiosity

and like the headless hare
you too lost yours

six feet of diamonds
rolled up in the freezer
and guts to vapor

your rattle
in the bowl with the others

i pick your bones
from my teeth
and think of how the rattlesnake runs

bustle

i thought about going to
China
but i saw a film
and
it was not of history
or legend

but rather
an industrialized
bustling
nation

all i could
see
or
hear
were the sounds
of traffic

the foreign horns tooting
like submissive mice getting ass fucked by fire ants
and
the gorgeous gray smog in the streets
so Christmasy

everyone
was in a blind hurry

cars
and
bicycles
and
rickshaws

and the poor
miserable
frozen
limited people
amassing the sidewalks

suddenly
i could not believe
so many

people
were in such a hurry
and
made such a life's effort
to get to some shit box sweat shop
just
to make
my
fucking
underwear

now that i know
i'll wear them more often
or
whenever the occasion
may call

score

you know the world is fucked
when your credit score
is bigger than you are

you're not a person anymore
you're a number
just like a convict

gotta piss bankman

go piss number

number goin piss bankman
number back from pissin bankman

back from pissin number

why you fuckin me bankman

bankman fuckin you good number

yessir
bankman fuckin me real good

everything is a function of currency
he used to say
probably still does

maybe that's why he doesn't function

maybe this world would work better
without greed

maybe

but i'll never know

bankman won't let me piss without payin

bye bye bankman

time

sometimes i have so much fun
i don't even remember having it

sometimes i have so much fun
i can't stop laughing about it

sometimes i have so much fun
i hurt someone that i love

and sometimes i have so much fun
i never want to have fun again
ever

these are definitely
the best of times

hugging that porcelain bowl
isn't just exhausting untimely unwanted exercise
it stamps your ticket paid

yeap

i reckon so

hair

i've got about 14 hairs on my dick
balls included
10 or so on my ass
30 to 40 on my face
6 or 7 on my chest
and a few on my back

added all together
the number's not even close
to the amount of hair on my ears
my nose
my eyebrows
and my toes

Doc says it's the Indian blood in me

getting older is so shameful sometimes

luckily
i don't really give a damn

if i did
i'd write a poem about it

behave

that really sounds
wonderful

a poem a day

i feel the same way
about defecating

wouldn't that be
fantabulous

a poem fall
such as
a snow fall
soft on the tongue
made to dissolve
away
forever

why try to piss
when you don't have to

it seams that the
meanings to it all
belong only to the others

and that's just
how it is

so go find your
real home
and forget about it

love thy

it's beautiful here
the river runs deep
the cave carved cliffs
climb high into the heavens

from the porch
deer graze as i watch
aoudad climb the steep slopes
stones tumble beneath their hoofs
and fall into the green water
as the large mouth bass
jump at my top water jig

a cool front moved in last night
punching a hole in the body bag
of summer heat
the drapes dance in the breeze
the dogs have stopped panting

and there are things of which i am certain

the fire will soon come again
God is always watching
and my only neighbor
is a blueblood chickenshit cocksucker
who
if starving to death
i would not allow to drink
the bloody sweat off my screaming hot turd

but i am commanded to love him
and so i do

i love that sorry bastard
with every cell in my body

and should he ever
grow the balls to confront me
i'll probably love him to death

difference

sometimes
alone
doesn't seem to be enough

there's not enough
alone
to fill the loneliness

so i substitute
booze
pills
weed
and soy sauce
to make up the difference

baseball games too
i watch them by the hundreds

but lately
the images on the screen
are far away from those in my head

sometimes i can't grasp
a single thought
they all mush like stew
sinking the one i need

all these thoughts
and none wanting to share

reckon that's the loneliest
that's when there is no sense
nothing to do but suffocate
drowning in the steamy stew

hoping my diet
either saves me
or kills me

just in time to discover all the lost truth

30 fishing poles

maybe not exactly 30
maybe more
maybe less

but it doesn't matter
what matters is
30 fishing poles
no reels
no line
no tackle
no bait

that's what matters
everything that's missing
reason mostly

poor old dumb bastard
just stealing to steal
falling in line
riding chaos
inhuman idiocy

30 fishing poles
maybe more
maybe less

maybe i'd a grabbed em
had it been me
and not that
poor old man

US

we were night fishing off the pier
the generator hummed from its wooden hive
the locomotive lights beamed down on our sunburned backs

i couldn't throw a fit
almost every cast
dealt a nasty bird's nest

fuck
i did it again

that's what your problem is
i finally figured it out

he was sitting down
readying his precious new cast net

figured what out

how to tell when you're stoned

how's that smart guy

you have no dexterity
you're a fucking bumbling idiot
look at you over there

mind your net
pussy boy

then he stood
and flung it spinning finely into Christmas Pass
but he forgot to hold on to the pull line
it sank quickly in the shining brown water

immediately he dove in
sort of a toe touch swan dive gut buster
it was beautiful and chivalrously hideous

i couldn't wait for him to surface

but when he did
his hairpiece was cockeyed

and water beaded off of it
as it does on wolf fur
or miniature drink umbrellas

grabbing the pier
he just looked up at me
befuddled and stoned

nice haircut
you fucking pothead

past due

my bills come stamped
in large red letters

past due

i show the bills to my ass
but no money comes out

maybe they should
change the stamp to
shit

maybe they should just
keep the bills
save the postage
and quit wasting their time

they're not wasting mine
i take care of that
myself

whatever you say

i choose to live my life
and nothing more

i am a simple child of God

my home is the earth
my limit is the sky
my mind is my engine
my heart my rudder

i must always remember this

people are
for the most part
kind

but really
they're a bunch of fucking thieves

you will steal nothing from me

your condemnation is useless
my imprisonment only
feeds more poison
to the ill fated
the world's toilet of people

it matters not what another says
nor what another does
nor another's power on this earth

stature and power
are foolish illusions

i try hard to remember this
and you should too

nice

the sun just broke this morning's cloud line
the river runs green and cold
the black brush and prickly pear dine on the fine sunshine
the dogs and cats sleep into their own mornings
the hills stand proud and rugged above the water

this glorious day Thy Lord hast given
glows selflessly upon us
and all i can think about is moustaches

bull's eye

my
moderation
lays
comatose
between
feast
and
famine

Mama Suzi

i just stopped to drop off
her warsh bucket

but she wouldn't have it

turn that thing off
come upstairs
i've got stew and pie
and Bill's here

told her i didn't
want to be a bother

turn that damn thing off
we got beer too

i had my whiskey bottle
and
you don't fuck with Mama Suzi

she claims boldly
her Ohio yankeeship
but insists she'll
whip ass like a Texan

i hadn't eaten in 2 days
it was the best stew
i've ever had
the company was kind and humble
another night in the mountains

now i'm doin some
Sunday whiskey wishin
having finished my bottle
over dinner

a fine
fine
dinner
indeed

cutie

i want to kill my dog
he's bothering the workmen
he barks and bites at their shovels

they said it doesn't bother them
he's just having fun

well he's driving me
out of my fucking mind

oh he ain't bothering us none
hell man i got five kids at home

how bout you drop him in that hole
and cover it up right quick

we couldn't do that to this cutie

he is a cutie too

i get the feeling
i ain't ever
gonna have to stop
shooting
them cuties

6/22/2009 6:21 PM – ok ranchito

bitchin

look for fairness in life
and you will find none

find a grain of justice
and you have discovered
the entire field

honesty
is a fucking joke

balls
are only for
bulls

and betrayal
is guaranteed

living good
has been
raped and murdered

it's sad
this part of life

that the only
truly
hateful thing
on earth
is
us

forgotten

one hangs in my mind

a web spun around my soul

at the top i love her smile
on the bottom
she gathers me
and pours me down
next to her
to warm
and to heal

and when i fight the world
and when i don't come home
and when i break and fall away
she accepts me
she understands

wrapped inside her
we survive in a shawl of lamb

fingers of ivy
rest soft on my broken skin
and i know that she loves all of me

it's what i really wanted
that woman i never had

i'll die alone now
maggots for the flesh
my grave full of bones
and a lovely woman
finally
forgotten

rude
fucking
cunt

moon watch

i fell into an
orange moon tonight

full it rose
mightily
over goat mountain

i watched it through my
binoculars
brightening white as it rose

my heart wanted to stop
or
i wanted it to

where the hell am i

and when will i find out

dirty hatred

i'm dirty. my boots are caked with dried mud from the tank. my hands are blistered and calloused. the space not consumed by the keloids are scabbed from cuts and swollen with deeply burrowed splinters. my spine feels as though it contains a right angle at the lumbar. a steady pain has pulsated inside my left hip for the last three months. i haven't slept for seven days, though on some nights i have passed-out several times for a few hours. two ingrown toenails have plagued my feet for six months. they're bothersome but not painful enough to tend to with resolution. beneath the mud my skin is as dry as sun-drenched newspaper. to keep from itching i work up a sweat. lotion seems to have a self-depleting quality so i don't waste my time or money. ironically enough, i have plenty of time to waste but no money on which to waste it. Max, my longhaired tabby, cries for attention at my feet. he wants me to stop writing, lean back in my chair so he can sleep on my belly. he's relentless. i've known no other cat as boisterous as Max. at the moment i want to grab him by his tail and sling him into the stone wall, or maybe stand and kick him into the fireplace. instead i scratch his head and gaze into his big green eyes asking politely, "please, for the love of all that is quiet, shut the fuck up." he meows again and rubs against my legs. how can i be so cruel as to turn away the face of love? insanity is strange. it smells like an opium den or a hot middle eastern morgue. when i can't take it any longer i go outside into the desert evening, drink whiskey and think of what it will be like when i die. the breeze is a broom that sweeps it all away. the mountains in the distance are my only friends. i light a fire in the pit but have nothing to cook. the flames, the breeze, the mountains, the raw smell of fresh air – it's home and all the pain and all the noise and all the blood is but a life in a body with no cares. as i sit and stroke the chest of the wolf, i wonder who it was that invented hatred and what purpose it has ever served.

no regrets

if
i
thought
of
all
the
time
i
wasted

i
wouldn't
have
the
time
to
waste
thinking
about
it

constant

people never change
he swears it

all they do is change
i swear back

liars
thieves
murderers
rapists
child molesters
tyrants
cannibals
visionaries
mama's boys
bluebloods
shit eaters
gang bangers
soccer moms
preachers
demons
tough guys
little dicks
war lords
revolutionaries
law men
satanic saints
vegetarians
blood drinkers
drunks
martyrs
pussies
poets
painters
pot smokers
and
people of God

there is no avoiding the world's only constant
there is only avoiding the people
that change never changes

question

how many ways
can i sabotage
my efforts to misbehave

in a drunken
stoned
slur
on any
God given
day of solitude and nature
and animals
and good people

i reckon
i could fuck it up
several times
or many times
but never
could i actually
completely resist

i don't want to
and this is a difficult
opponent
with which to compete

thanksgiving
has been the easiest one
a blackout mulligan
if you will

then there's the

but i've been up all night
i couldn't sleep

give me something
that will help me
nap today

just a couple hours
maybe three in a row
but that sounds

too exciting

and beer is good
for a sour tummy
she once said

and it is
and so are the rest
and so is the scotch
and the everything
stirred into the slur

i shouldn't do
that
which feels
absolutely
certain
that i should

trust in whom

i have faith
in the natural order
of things

it's often sad
and frustrating

much like
i imagine
constipation
to be

3/22/2009 4:41 PM – ok

smoke

i'm 43 years old
i live in a barn
i have bad credit
and i'm so broke i couldn't rent
a used rubber off the floor of a Mexican whorehouse
and my only neighbor is a self indulgent cocksucker

but things could be worse
i know because they usually get that a way
just when i think i've hit bottom
i fall further down the hole

so i lean hard on my faith in God
bathe in the clear water of the Devil's River
and sip lightly on my bottle of rubbing alcohol

but my mother still loves me
the sun still shines fine
and life keeps moving on

blessings sometimes hide behind the hell in life
you just have to push forward
praying that you'll come out of it
without even the smell of smoke

that's smoke as in hell fire
not pot smoke

that's something completely different
and
i'll take
either
or

going for broke

i
finally
made
it

big time

leaving on

echoes call again
this place empties
things go here and there
the echoes resonate longer
and i grow more anxious
a bit older
more curious of my place in tomorrow

it's sad going away again
knowing there will be no return is delicate
but the spirit of the west winds
whispers my name and i must go

shoving off will be quick and silent
drifting away in the darkness
leaving tears for the others if they choose
for i believe we really never part

it's not easy
it never has been
but from the quiet flight comes the goodness
the adjuvant struggles will serve my awakening well
and beyond the night awaits another beginning

i will forget no one
each of you my blessings

it is not your fault
it is mine because i cannot
escape the whisper

my heart leads and i must follow
you will all be with me forever
God will see this through

goodbyes are unnecessary
the memories give me strength
helping me trail through another virgin passage

and should ever we gather again
you will have never been away

funny

all this way you came
all your struggles
all your broken hearts
all the misunderstandings
all the wasted time
all the gutless fucking pain

wasted time on
pure insecurity
mindless jealousy
godless greed

and then
straight to your own grave

kind of funny
ain't it

career

sometimes
like right now
i wonder why i decided to become a writer
instead of a doctor or a rocket scientist

my pay is horrible if any
my writer friends are broke brilliant drunk losers
my dogs eat better than i do
and everything in the world is a fucked up mystery
that has to be contemplated to no end

but let the truth be told

i love the life
i love the freedom
i love the thoughts
the words
the laughter
the booze
the drugs
the hangovers
the fires
the music
the sky
the women sometimes
the rambling
fucking girls with mohawks and dirt under their fingernails
but mostly
i love
completely submitting
to the imprisoning freedom

besides
no matter how hard
i cheated
i just could not pass college algebra

pajaro

birdman
got drunk last night
he passed out
in the middle
of a rocky mountain road

the folks around here
are kind
and
look out for one another

when birdman awoke
he knew that goodness too

it was glowing in the color
orange

safety orange
i believe it's called

as in road hazard orange

you've seen it

just as he did
as he spit the dust from his mouth
and gathered his bearings

sitting squarely
between
two
orange
rubber
safety cones

grateful
to all these kind folks

6/22/2009 12:04 PM – ok

thread

i can't imagine a better time
to suicide

all the excuse are here

homeless
penniless
nowhere to go
the essence of burden

it's perfect

but something strange burns me
i still feel
the need to hang on

something
won't stop
fighting back

it's not me
i'm fried

it is faith
it is stronger than i
it endures much more than i
it is ruthless
it is real

empty of all things this world
and i've never before felt
the warming strength of
God's presence
like i do
right now

con per miso

enjoy every moment of your life
smile at adversity
laugh at pettiness
bless em instead of curse em
be the person God meant you to be
be open
be gracious
be glorious
help someone
think about the ones you love
and the ones that have chosen to love you
fight evil to the death
be righteous always
walk miles in the shoes of every other
speak when you have something to say
otherwise
listen with great devotion
find the peace that's missing
always look farther than you can see
open and reach out your hands
stop for a moment
study
inhale with your mind
know what you have
get what you don't
be the essence of humility
sail in the winds of the stars
and bask in the fine morning moonshine
roll the dice of life through the mountains
dive down for the sand dollars of the sea
listen to lovely music and let it stir your soul
seek out the melodies and play them if you can
spread the harmony as if it were your world
try hard when you can and harder when you can't
stay joyous in the good times and more so in the bad

because
one day
your heart will stop beating
and you'll be forced to live only on the seeds of your soul

cards

spent the previous day writing hot checks
finally got enough fuel for the trip

drove to Uvalde first thing this morning

pulling into docs office parking lot
my phone rings
its the doc

sorry
but my brother in law
had a heart attack yesterday
i'm not seeing patients today
but
i can
see you in a month

fuck me
fuck you
and fuck your brother in law

turned around
went to a Mexican dive
ate a breakfast
that they should have served me
in the bathroom

216 miles

send em
down the sewer
with the rest of the turds
as the man once said

i swear
somethin's gotta give

soon

6/28/2009 3:06 PM – ok

one for the non believers

where
did
where
come
from

winged

for lack of a more
pure word
angels
pounce this hell on earth

they show
and they shine
in the darkest of hours

they're not the government
they're not the shiny smiles
and they're not
the ones
who claim prophecy

fuck those people

if you don't
they will definitely
fuck you

evil bleeds darkness
it finds the weakness
in you
and murders all hope

don't let it happen
focus on the light

their wings are silent
but they are real

doubt them
and you nurse the life
of demons

trust in them
and let the light
guide
your lost soul

sobriety

i've been sober
for 23 years

i've been sober for 19

i've been

okay
good for you
you needed it

but i don't need it
thrown in my face
stuffed down my throat
stabbed in my back

congratulations
you're still a fuck

sober or not

i haven't been sober
ever

probably die this way

who knows

no one here

guarantee me
tomorrow
and i might lay off
for a while
and watch it go by

until then
bite me

representative

only people can
be the most horrible
of witches

they'll do anything
to do nothing

i've never been much on
returning phone calls
but that's
not
what i get paid to do

but you do

your sorry ass
get's paid
to make calls
between me
the adjuster
and the mechanic

but you're fucking lazy
and do none of this

the only call you retuned
was the one in which
i requested your supervisor

he sounds like a worm in a hole
maybe he'll crawl out and call me
maybe i'll get that sorry witch
fired

i've always disliked
the insurance industry
now i remember why

they're out to receive checks
not send them
it's a gutless
cowardice
license to steal

so get your cock out
and
use it to your advantage

it's just
fire
against
fire

burn em
bury em
and move on down the road

bastard

i'm quite certain
that if i
am to reap
all
that i have sown

some good

the rest
mostly bad

i'd just as soon
live forever

the blathering

i feel like i'm cheating you
if i'm not kicking your balls in as you read this
i'm also uncertain how real
i can make this experience
through the wonderment of the written word
the only way i know how is to stick to the truth
so that's what follows
the truth
the absolute gospel
according to me truth
names changes
legal stuff
etcetera

I want to see her again. She's such a pleasant surprise. - Blaze Foley

It's not your company that I mind. It's you. - Unknown

keep pumping it in
just keep pumping
pump hard and fast
make your legs tremble with atrophy
concentrate on what you're doing
do it harder
faster
bury it
more
it takes more
keep going
keep pumping it in
the end will come
if you work hard enough
and remember
no one likes a quitter

so i kept going
whatever was there was soon ingested
it didn't matter
anything
preferably the good stuff
but i'm a beggar
among other things
asshole mainly

whores

the world is
full of whores
and greedy fools

nothing is without
a price

you're always
paying for it

one way or another

you're always
paying for it

i pay to watch
a television
that advertises to me

i'm so fucking stupid
that i pay
for people
to sell me their shit

i pay duty
every time
i buy something
isn't that enough

it is for me

and you whores
you greedy fools
you'll never die

you're simply not
deserving enough

fly

if you suck at something
quit doing it

find something you're worth a shit at
that's right
at
that's what i said

anywho
give that something a try
if you're still terrible
move on

think of what gives you an erect soul
if something bites you in the ass
and i mean rattler style
fire
no smoke
just pain
give it a whirl
you never know

but you ain't Johnny Cash
and i ain't Oscar Wilde

and nothing is more confusing than soul searching

the old man used to say

you get bit by a rattlesnake
you better bite that sumbitch back

i didn't really get it
until i actually did bite back
but that's what he meant
hard lesson learned

that was a joke
which part i am uncertain

ryan says
hard times are in the middle road
for us all

he's right
so turn to the sky and fly
hard into the sunrise

you'll never get away
but you sure as hell
didn't waste the trip

713

just this morning
i was looking
at the only photograph
that i have of his son

what a big kid
he looks like trouble
i hope to meet him some day

daddy said

if it was just the girl
i'd be gone already
but
i'm not
lettin go of my boy

we asked one another

why do
they
have to have the chaos
the calamity
the heretic drama

it's such a waste of time

why can't they just
be happy

hell
he said
i'm happy just
having a few beers
smoking some pot
watching tv
taking zanax
and
letting the world
go by

why
must we

waste this precious time

he didn't know
either

Trapper was a handsome mix of German Shepherd and wolf. he was ignored as a puppy and as a result was wild and did not warm to people well, much less other animals. i took him in and over the years tried my best to change him. i thought that i had.

Big Guy was a beautiful large black cat with gold eyes. my ex-wife brought him home one day. he was six weeks old and tiny. she named him Joshua. i hate that name so i call him Big Guy. after our divorce his name officially became Big Guy. as a young tomcat he fought his way through many nights. he was a great hunter of birds and snakes and squirrels. one day he fought a dog. he survived, but was neutered immediately thereafter. at the age of nine he was a black ball of sleeping muscle.

10.17.3 – 7:50 PM – Carrizal

dead animals

Trapper killed Big Guy tonight
probably with a little help
from the others

this is the wolf's way
but the bloody scratches
were on Trapper's hazel eyes
Big Guy lay just inside
stiff and lifeless and cold

at dusk
i buried Big Guy
near the house
and covered his shallow grave
with large rocks
his crucifix is temporary
tomorrow
i'll make a more appropriate one

actually i'll make two
Trapper's dead too

i held him by the collar
as he smiled up at me
and shot him in the head

i held his quivering body
until it lay still

beneath the cold moonlight
i buried Trapper
about a half a mile southwest of the Carrizal

the brains
the bloodstained rug
both their food bowls
my gloves
and every stitch of clothing
i had been wearing
burned in a large fire
where Trapper's blood had spilled

i'm sorry God
i waited
before killing him
it was not out of anger
it was all that i could do
please take them into Your arms
i'll forever love and miss them

it's been a tough day

sweet dreams

return

i got the stink
on me

she went
somewhere
better

now i'm just
the same thing
she came back to

you
try
try
try

then you
cry
cry
cry

fuck you
if you can't
live by your
own rules

strike

to this point
in my life
nothing
not even
the swollen seas
elucidates to me
the great might
of God
as the fat white lightning
striking
the ground
before me

scorching our
sweet
sweet
earth

don't
ever
be
foolish
enough
to
think
you're
the one
in charge

ever

wind

in my dreams
i'm always chasing something
but there are always obstacles
that first
must be overcome

as i race about
people interfere
needing something from me
keeping me from the chase

last night
i had to catch a plane to London
a private plane waiting for me to climb aboard

but i lost my bag
i lost my drugs
i couldn't find my whiskey bottle
i wore borrowed wrinkled clothes

and at the farewell party
i had to stop and greet friends and family
all who were long dead and gone
their skin blue
their dress formal
their hugs cold
their smiles eternal

i rushed about
but didn't make the plane in time

while pissing my morning void
i screamed in anger

i'm not going to London today damnit

i laid back down on the couch
the wind blew cold and moist through the windows
the dogs barked at boats passing up river

God
will you give me one hour of dreamless sleep

as i dozed
the jet's engines whined
waiting for its final passenger
and the party still went on

God said no
you're too late
you've wasted your time with the chase
if you worked this hard in your waking hours
you just might be worth a shit
get up and carry on with your chase

i penned the word fart on an unpaid bill
and walked out into the morning mist

chase it
redeem your time
it's limited

do this now

when you're grounded
you'll have plenty of time to fly

but i do

the moon is big
a white shining ring draping it
the neat scotch
a fine single malt
sent in the mail
by an old friend
in new york city

i've stretched 3 days
out of the bottle
but 4 ain't gonna happen
not tonight

the wind
will blow the morning in
the moon will wane in purple flame
and the sun
will bring fired life
into the morning sky
just as i awaken to take a shit

i am uncertain
if i am
fearless
or
just
without
control
or concern

fuck
who cares

now

i am amazed by other people's logic
it's what fascinates me
it is my paycheck

i take it to the Bank of Life
and tell them
give me my fucking cash
now

because that's when it happens
now

not in the morning
not when a commercial comes
or
when you come

now

right now

7/6/2009 9:33 PM – ok

in love

to know
is to fuck

then ask yourself

in any way
do i
still
want to be here

if
in any sense
yes
be the answer

you're
probably
still just
horny

mulligan

to sell
a sliver
of the soul
is to sell
the whole soul

the soul
does not bend
but it does break

a crack is a gorge

a drip
all the oceans and seas

nothing is free
nothing is plentiful
nothing is infinite

nothing goes
unknown

the soul sees
to this

it is all that is real
it is all that will last

mine will be heavily
scarred
but it will not be
rejected

that being said
i wish you well

candle

what do you do
when the world
has no meaning

where is the reasoning
the catalyst for motivation
activity
progress
something

Townes said it about an old man
he'd met in Houston

just waiting around to die

and it seems like
dying is the easy part
the waiting is the real torture

but suicide
will ruin everything

that's what it does
leaves you in that nasty barren hole
with nothing but eternity
to wait for

and it comes
like a pro
nothing shot everywhere
all over you

you can't feel it
you can't feel anything

it's just more
of what you left behind

except
any hope at all

nine

God keeps sending me angels
and i don't know why

i just lean on Him
and He carries me

the days come and go
the nights are quiet and cool

i can feel the fat around my waist
jiggle when i walk
so i quit walking so much

now i feel the fat jiggle when i drive
but i do drive
a big old dirty truck

it beats walking jiggling fat

something can always beat something

someone has it worse

then another has it even worse

then
well
well
then

just watch out
you don't get too big
to carry

cause nine is it
that's all you get

angels in groups of ten
are meant
for the humblest of men

7/17/2009 11:38 AM –ok

thanks

i finally found
a use
for all my bills

i stack them
upside down
next to my head
wherever i sleep

with a pen
clipped
to the collar of my
t shirt
and my headlamp
nearby

i'm ready to write
at any moment i might awake

it's worked pretty good
for some twenty five years now

the more delinquent
i become
the more canvas they mail me

so i just want to say
to all those kind
companies

fuck you
and
thanks
for all that free paper

liar

truth is not selective
it has no conscience
it has no agenda
it has nothing but itself

truth is purity
it is birds in flight
it is a sky of light
it is fearless
and proudly humble

men think they can manipulate
truth
they believe
altered truth will dissolve and vanish
but it will not

truth cannot be changed
its strength is beyond men
its honor is bound in nature
it's life everlasting

run from truth
and you finish in absolute futility
as it patiently awaits you at the end

cowardly men cry foul
their lies are of no use
these miserable foul fools of the earth

i gave it to you
you think that you have succeeded in your evasion
but you are a royal fool
a king among sinners and thieves

your day is coming
mine too

despise me if you wish
but i'm so happy that i'm not you
soul selling is for the consumers of evil
the spineless men of stature
the spilling blood of hollow money

the weak
the cruel
the truly lonely ones

it's coming
all names will be called
and
when your number is up
you're done

but it's not too late

look into the eyes of a child
bite into the heart of the buffalo
listen to the natives sing
watch the embers rise away
dance in the glory of the fire
sleep in dark dreamless night

look me in the eye
come clean

do it now
doing it later is too late

truth is all merciful
painful
difficult
easy
incriminating
and above all
life giving

try it
live it
die in its arms

you have nothing to lose
except your lost soul
and i too
will be there
if you need me

saint Jude

(make your petition)

how could i ask
for anything more

i just wanted to say

thanks

4/6/03 10:48 PM – Carrizal

spade

sleep is precious
it comes at 10:00 pm
and ends at 11:00 pm
sometimes midnight

under the hold of insomnia
for months now

at first i hated it
fought it in futility
now it is my life

the moon glows brighter
and the sun rises faster
but i miss nothing

maybe i will stop sleeping
all together

it does nothing
but interrupt my life's process

the wilderness is awake
so am i
so is God

only the cats seem to find sleep
and i can live off their slumber
i can pull it into me
because it's deep

it deprives them of nothing
but energizes me with will
and more time to question and live

the flies still dance in my peripheral
on the other side
i wonder why people lie
i wonder if i really do have friends

question my integrity
and you cut your own throat

our relationship will bleed to death
as i walk away forever

a man is his word

if his word is false
then he is nothing
but a poor lost soul
who needs the hand of God
for
he will no longer have mine

if you lie
then you cheat
and
steal by proxy

your weakness is a call
that you have chosen to ignore

i'll ignore you now

the stars seek my attention
they are true
and
i too
will ignore them
when they call me
a spade

jump

the closest
i've come to flying
is snow skiing
taking a jump
while racing down the mountain
the bigger the better
commonly resulting
in a massive
crash of twisted
skis and snowy
falling
chaos
and
of course
some asshole
screaming

nice choke buddy

and i didn't even know him
spontaneously rude
i reckon

flying doesn't feel like
falling off a house
or off a horse
or out of a tree
or into a fire
or off bar stools
or off your own feet
down the rocky slopes
of summertime

i've tried

and i've flown
in small airplanes
it's like riding bitch
on your neighbor's
riding lawn mower
but i've always wanted
to jump out of an airplane

i just
can't decide
if
i want a parachute
or not

5/28/2009 8:22 PM – ok

the ok ranch

the ok
ain't ok
anymore

this road
is a dead end
for a reason

it's made for
money shitters
greenhorns
bluebloods
and
people with plush
green lawns
and
clean
white skin

my skin is red
my pockets
empty
my river
running dry

everything i own
is for sale

except my soul

Jesus owns that

and that's
the only thing
that's still ok
at the ok

okay

yesterday

was hard
it was very difficult
i did nothing
not one thing
and it was hard
it was very difficult to stay alive

for freedom also comes to the evil thoughts
the ones with swollen fat legs
and over inflated asses
they won't move out of the way
and you have no place else to look
but at all that swollen dirty skin

yesterday was quite difficult
i was unsure if i would last
it makes me tired

i'm tired
Lord i'm tired

it's over now
and i made it through the night
and through the day
and into another bout with bad thoughts
bloody thoughts
thoughts not good
thoughts with fat bloody stumps
that won't move out of the way

and only sleep brings peace
the days are lost in half forgotten memories
i fall into the nights
drunk and foul and numb

that's how it's done

leave early
get shitfaced
before you come home

7 dead Paisanos

sevens everywhere

i drink seven beers
then seven scotches
i smoke seven joints
and watch seven ballgames
i twist seven wire crosses
and wear a seven inch cock
really
really
hard
i have seven male animals
a vet appointment on the seventh
and seven dollars in my pocket
2 in quarters

today i fished out
seven dead Paisanos
from the stock tank
on top of the bluff

2 mamas
2 papas
3 younguns

seven

i laid them out on the rocks
there would be no digging
just drying and decaying in the sun

i've watched the process as it works
and it does work
every time

they die
they rot
they disappear
then another one falls
and six more with it
it's depressing sometimes
sometimes seven times as much

someone said it was a lucky number
someone says lots of stuff

i know luck
is not real

but
still
i
wonder

what about the sevens

1/15/2006 7:54 PM – mckoetting

sartorial thief

it's not really stealing
we're a community
me and him
the years define it

so
he can do strange stuff

lie to me
trick me into thoughts superfluous
of sickness in my family

why
why

what's wrong with these fucking people

why is it so difficult
to
mind your own business

i don't call you
i don't call you back
i don't invite you here
or anywhere
but still you show

more miserable each time

and you said we
weren't going to town
you said it for sure

4 times total
each time for you
each time for no reason
why are you acting like a
big gay queer incestuous conniving intrusive weird fuck

and dating my old girlfriend
and fleeing with my only windbreaker
and yelling at me
in my own fucking house

fill me full of steak and scotch
then take me back to my fire in the desert
and leave me to my lacunal fall

you knew it was coming
hell
you paid for it
even told me so
several times

saturday night
thanksgiving weekend
60 thousand acres
swirling in warm firelight
and

shut the fuck up

just what
in the fuck
do you think
you're thinking

it's disturbing

both
your overly odd behavior
and
that such strange things
find their way to me

when other things
peaceful things
just pass me by
in the darkness

in a year

sober
or
dead
or
right
back
here
again

idiot

outside my door
2 stoned idiots
are working
on my house

there's Mexican music
on the radio

there's a steady breeze
through the mountain pines

there's an even steadier stream
of mayo licked
bullshit
raging above
any sounds of God

one idiot has 2 teeth
and a scar on his scalp
from when some pissed off
Korean
shot him in the head
he got pissed
at that Korean
and kilt him dead

idiot number 2
is shooting for
d u i
number 6
he looks of cancer
and prison
and he talks very loud
and he talks a lot

but as i sit up here
and listen to them
pass the day

i drink my whiskey
lick the mayo
and read about
idiot number 2

in the local rag

it was a car theft ring
a kangaroo court fiasco
the crime never happened
all charges
dropped

except for idiot number 1
he's going to jury trial

but it may be a while
cause
idiot number 1
ain't in the computer
and all his possessions
fit comfortably
in his back pocket
of his other britches
that might be real
but probably not

he tries to buy
2 beers from me every day
i give him the beer
and he shits in my toilet
and he might steal my truck
but probably not

and i'm writing a poem about it
and
wondering
who's
the
real
idiot
here

windex

my mother always told me

spray windex on it
it takes the stinger out

she carried it in her car
spraying it on the red skin blotch
she said

that'll pull that stinger right outta there

and it did
and sometimes
on the way home from school
we would stop for ice cream
peppermint fudge ribbon
nothing stung after that

30 years later it still works

i just tried to brush him away
but he got pissed
and stung me on the neck
but i didn't let it interrupt
my game of fetch with Scotty

i sprayed it on
it's purple now
the windex
but the stinger's gone
sucked right outta there

and the windows are dirty
a half moon over
Texas
i can still see the light
and no bee's ever gonna get me
not get me for good

hope not

www.ingramcontent.com/pod-product-compliance
Lightning Source LLC
La Vergne TN
LVHW091159080426
835509LV00006B/754